Broken Shields

A GROUNDWOOD BOOK

Text and design copyright © 1994 by Claudia Burr, Krystyna Libura and Ma. Cristina Urrutia
Translation copyright © 1997 by Groundwood Books Ltd.
Originally published in Mexico as *Escudos rotos* by Ediciones Tecolote 1994
First English language edition 1997

The publisher gratefully acknowledges the assistance of the Canada Council and the Ontario Arts Council.

Printed and bound in China by Everbest Printing Co. Ltd.

Groundwood Books / Douglas & McIntyre
585 Bloor Street West, Toronto, Ontario M6G 1K5

Distributed in the U.S.A. by Publishers Group West
4065 Hollis Street, Emeryville, CA 94608

Library of Congress data is available.

Canadian Cataloguing in Publication Data
Burr, Claudia
Broken shields
"A Groundwood book".
Translation of: Escudos rotos
Spanish text based on Historia general de las cosas de Nueva Espana, book XII, in the Florentine Codex by Fray Bernardino de Sahagun. Images taken from Historia de las Indias by Diego Duran.
ISBN 0-88899-303-X (bound) ISBN 0-88899-304-8 (pbk.)
1. Mexico - History - Conquest, 1519-1540 - Juvenile literature. 2. Aztecs - Juvenile literature. I. Libura, Krystyna. II. Urrutia, Ma. Cristina (Maria Cristina). III. Aldana, Patricia, 1946- . IV. Sahagun, Bernardino V. Duran, Diego, d. 1588? Historia de las Indias de Nueva Espana e Islas de Tierra Firme. VI. Title.
F1230.B8713 1997   j972'.02   C97-930468-7

Let us sing our grief,
let us lament our fate
so that no one will ever forget
what our people have suffered,
when they came,
when they subjugated us, there in
Tenochtitlan, they the Spaniards.

Broken Shields

Text and design by Claudia Burr, Krystyna Libura and Maria Cristina Urrutia

Before the Spaniards came,
and even as the sun shone,
a huge comet fell
announcing their arrival.

The Year One Cane arrived and the Spaniards appeared. Suddenly they were there, near our shore, where the sky joins the sea.

And when Moctezuma heard this,
he immediately sent messengers,
as if he believed, as if he thought
that it was our god Quetzalcóatl
returning to us.

And a woman from
here, one of us,
was their interpreter.
She was called Malintzín.
They had captured her,
there on the coast.

And when they finally moved, when the Spaniards advanced, the people of the coast guided them, led them, prepared the way for them.

From then on
Moctezuma had
no sleep, no food.
He was afraid,
he was uneasy
about the future
of his people.

And when the Spaniards
arrived at the land
of Tlaxcala, the chiefs
of that people
came to greet them.
They showed them
their palaces.
They took care of them.
They helped them.

Soon the Spaniards took the road to Mexico.

They were covered with steel, dust blew around them.

Their metal lances, their bat-shaped lances, shone like the sun.

And then Moctezuma came out to meet them, to greet them with splendid gifts.

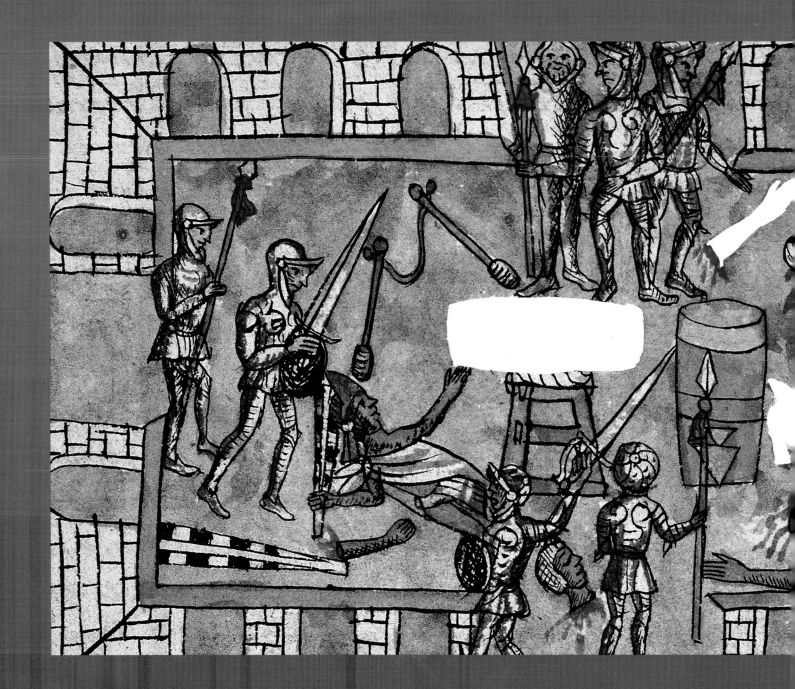

And when the time came
to celebrate the feast of the gods,
when there was dancing and singing,
then the Spaniards appeared.
They blocked all the doorways.
They cut off the hands of the
 drummers.
They cut off
their heads.

Their heads rolled far
from their bodies.

In this way,
the war began.
The Spaniards
tried to flee the city
that night.
We followed them
and it was then
that we killed them.
Many died,
many drowned in
the canals.

The Spaniards
hid in Tlaxcala.
There they rested, fortified themselves.
They built brigantines.
Then, suddenly, they attacked
us again,
they surrounded us
by land,
and by water.

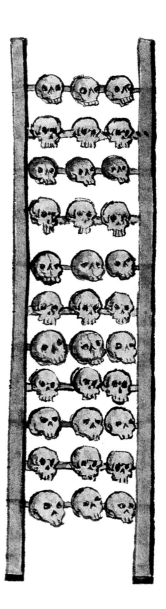

And once it happened
that our brave warriors
captured many Spaniards.
We took them to the altar,
we sacrificed them to the gods,
and their skulls were placed
on long poles, beside the temple.

grasas,

patio

palizaaa

æcalaunas.

For three months
we fought.
We suffered,
we were hungry.
We ate anything
we could find:
lizards, swallows
and corn husks.
We chewed water lilies,
leather and
dust from bricks.

And when they defeated us,

when we lowered our shields,

when we fell,

it was Three House

in the calendar of years,

and One Serpent

in the calendar of days.

This first-person account of the tragic downfall of the Ancient Mexicans is drawn from volume XII of Friar Bernardino de Sahagún's twelve-volume *A General History of the Things of New Spain*, published in the sixteenth century. It is based on his conversations with Mexicans who had been present at the events, and takes the form of a lament. The pictures come from *The History of the New Spanish Indies and Mainland Islands* by Friar Diego Durán. They were probably painted by Natives educated by the Spaniards.

IMPORTANT TERMS AND DEFINITIONS

brigantines–small light boats built by the Spaniards

Hernán Cortés–the leader of the Spaniards

Malintzín–Cortés's interpreter; the Spaniards called her La Malinche

Mexicans–the people who lived in and around Tenochtitlan, also called Ancient Mexicans or Aztecs

Moctezuma–the leader of the Mexicans

Quetzalcóatl–the plumed serpent and god of the Mexicans who had left his people and was supposed to return from the East

Tenochtitlan–the capital of Mexico, which was built on islands in the middle of a lake

Three House–1521, the year of the destruction of the Aztec empire by the Spaniards

Tlaxcala–a city and home of Moctezuma's bitter enemies (the Tlaxcalans) who helped the Spaniards defeat the Mexicans